Rahmah

The Woman Who Lived Without Food

A GREEN FIG BOOK

ILLUSTRATED BY RABYA GAYE

Green Fig

Dear Kids

We hope you enjoy this picture book! The drawings in this book are artistic depictions of events. This means how the illustrator imagined some of what happened at that time and not how they were in reality because we don't know how they truly looked.

Name: ....

Publisher: Green Fig
Pennsylvania, USA
www.gogreenfig.com

Note to Parents & Educators

Green Fig is happy to bring to our young readers the story of ***Rahmah, The Woman Who Lived Without Food*** from our rich Islamic heritage. Rahmah Bint Ibraheem is a real character who lived in the third Hijri century in Hazarasp (Persian for thousand horses), now known as Hazorasp or Khazarasp in Uzbekistan. Her story and what happened to her after her husband's martyrdom is documented in detail by the scholars such as Al-Hakim in his book "History of Nishapur".

This story showcases many matters; the truthfulness of the Religion of Islam, the honor of the martyrdom, and the extraordinary matters that God bestows on some pious people, among others. The matter that we wanted to highlight in this story is a very important one: it is that God is the Creator of the causes and their effects, and that a cause does not create its usual effect. Only Allāh creates. This means that an effect can happen without its usual normal cause and that a cause would not lead to a certain usual effect if God did not will so. That's why Rahmah did not get sick or die when she did not eat. God, The All-Mighty, preserved her body when she was alive without any nourishment. God has the power to create good health without the normal reasons for that. Prophet Jesus, peace be upon him, lives in the second heaven like angels do without eating or drinking and he is still alive. He is more than 2000 years old! Likewise, the huge fire did not burn Prophet Abraham, peace be upon him, when he was thrown in it. On the contrary, it was cool and safe on him, although usually, the fire burns. However, the fire does not create the burning and God did not will for that fire to cause burning to Prophet Abraham. God did not create the burning in Abraham from that fire. Similarly, when the knife was passed on the neck of Ishmael, peace be upon him, it did not cut him. If the knife creates cutting it would have cut his neck. It was a sharp knife; the same knife did cut the thicker neck of a big sheep that descended from Paradise.

We hope that your child will benefit from reading this story and we are happy to hear from you at info@gogreenfig.com

Green Fig Publishers

Hundreds of years ago, a young woman called Rahmah lived in the city of Hazarsap, along the road of caravans.

Rahmah lived with her husband and children.
Her husband was a poor wood carpenter
who gets his living day by day.

In Hazarasp there is a river that passes the big valley of <u>J</u>ayhūn. It gets very cold in there during the long winter season.

The big river freezes in this valley and becomes like a bridge that pack animals and even people with their carriages are able to cross. The thickness of the ice can reach up to twenty handspans if the winter is severe!

One winter day, a bad unjust king with 3000 horsemen crossed the icy river to invade the city. The people of Hazarasp asked for help by building a fire that could be seen from a faraway distance to signal that they are in danger. Before help arrived, some young men including Rahmah's husband, went outside the city's fortress to defend their people.

They fought bravely. They fought until their bows were cut, but they were outnumbered by the enemy. Most of them were killed or wounded.

The next day, help arrived. When the enemy saw the black flags of the Muslim's army and heard the sound of their tambourines, they fled away. Around 400 men from Hazarasp were dead. Rahmah's husband was among them.

Rahmah started crying. Family and neighbors came over to support her in her grief.

Her children were too young to understand
what happened. They were hungry and
asking for bread.

What is she going to do?!
Her husband left them no money.

Then, Ra_hmah heard the call for
Maghrib's prayer. Despite her sorrow,
she went and prayed. Ra_hmah was
a patient woman who found relief in
prayers. While she was prostrating
and making supplication (dua')
for Allāh to help her and help her
orphaned children, she fell asleep.

In her sleep, she saw a beautiful dream! She saw she was searching for her husband in a beautiful land that she has never seen before. A man called her and asked her where she is going. She said that she is looking for her husband. He told her to go to the right.

There, she saw a green land with splendid palaces and buildings so beautiful that she could not describe! She saw rivers that flow on the surface of this land.

She saw men with glowing faces wearing green clothes sitting in circles eating. These were the men who died as martyrs that day.

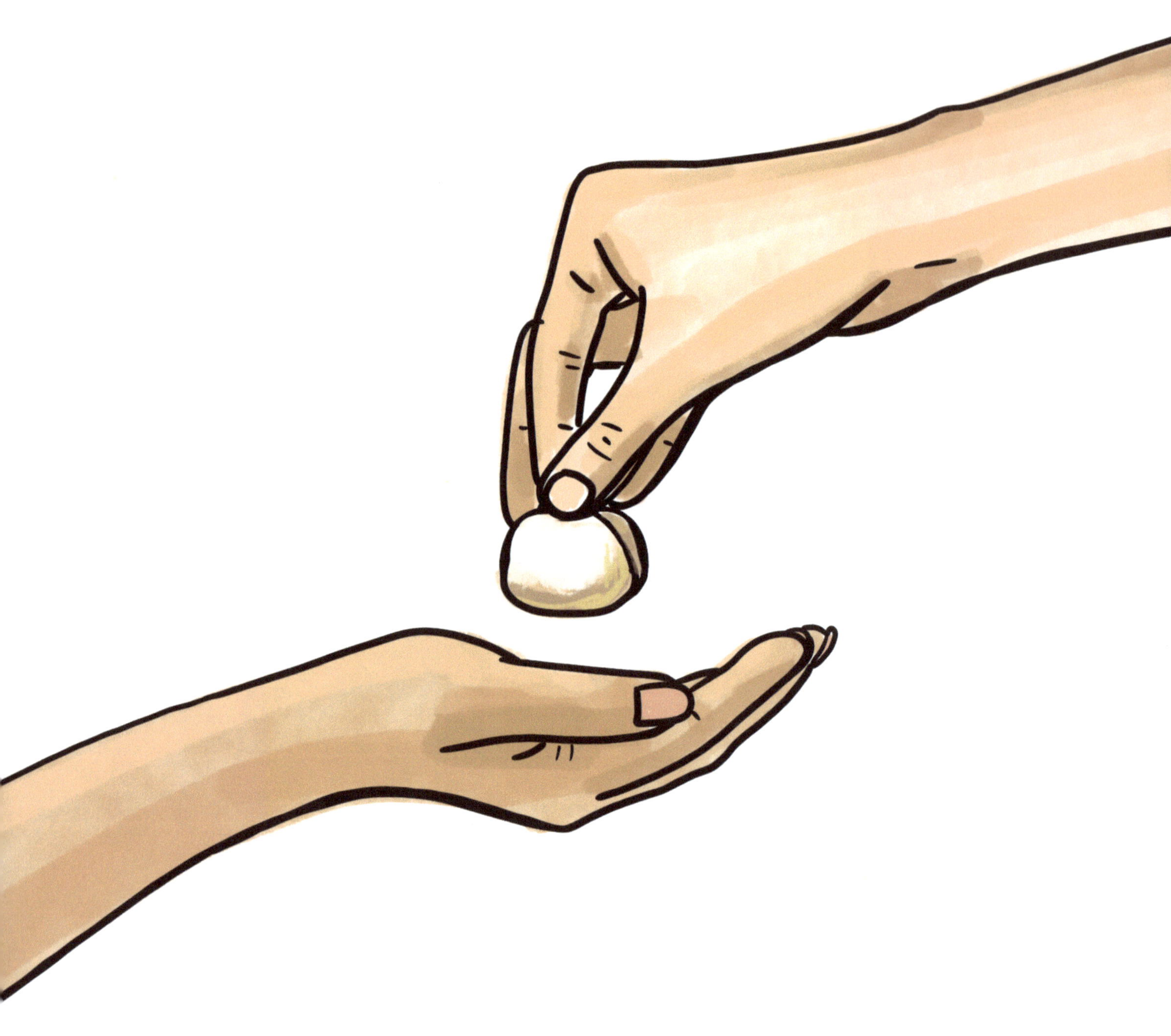

Rahmah looked carefully to see if her husband was among them. He saw her before she saw him. He called to her,"O Rahmah". She turned towards the familiar voice and saw her husband. His face was like the moon. He asked his friends' permission to give her a piece of bread since she was hungry and did not eat anything that day. He offered her a tiny piece of bread.

The bread was whiter than snow, sweeter than honey, and softer than butter. Rahmah ate the piece of bread. Then her husband told her, "Go, may God spare you the need of food and drink as long as you are alive in this world."

Rahmah woke up from her sleep feeling full and content. She never needed to eat or drink after that for the rest of her life. With time, her stomach got stuck to her back, so she used to tie a bag full of cotton to her belly to straighten up.

Despite not eating or drinking, she was energetic and was able to walk long distances in the fields around her town. She lived happy with her children and stayed healthy without any food for more than twenty years.

A Lesson from this Story

God is the Creator of everything. He created causes and the effects that result from these causes. He created food and created satiety upon eating it. He created fire and the burning upon touching it. God is the Creator of all causes and their effects; causes do not create their effects. God created the bread and made it a cause for satiety. So, it is God who created the satiety not the bread.

Food and drink are causes to maintain good health but not the creators of good health. Most people, if they eat and drink, their body and strength would be maintained because God made a cause ordinarily connected to its effect. However, God can create extraordinary matters so that a cause is present but its effect does not occur because God did not will for it to happen.

God willed for Rahmah to be in good health and not feel hungry or thirsty despite her not eating or drinking for the remainder of her life. In this story, there is a lesson for the believers that God is the One who creates good health and has the power to give someone a strong body without eating or drinking for the time that God willed. If food and drink create health, Rahmah's body, strength, and mind would not have been preserved for such a long time, around 30 years!

Fill the table with the usual effect corresponding to each cause using the words below. Bear in mind that a cause does not necessarily lead to its usual effect. As a miracle, the fire did not cause burning to Prophet Abraham when he was thrown into it because God did not will for the burning to occur to Abraham by this fire. Also, the same medication does not cure the same disease when taken by different people.

Cutting - Satiety - Health - Cure - Burning - Hunger - Thirst

Cause	Usual Effect
Bread	
Lack of food	
Nourishment	
Fire	
Knife	
Lack of water	
Medication	

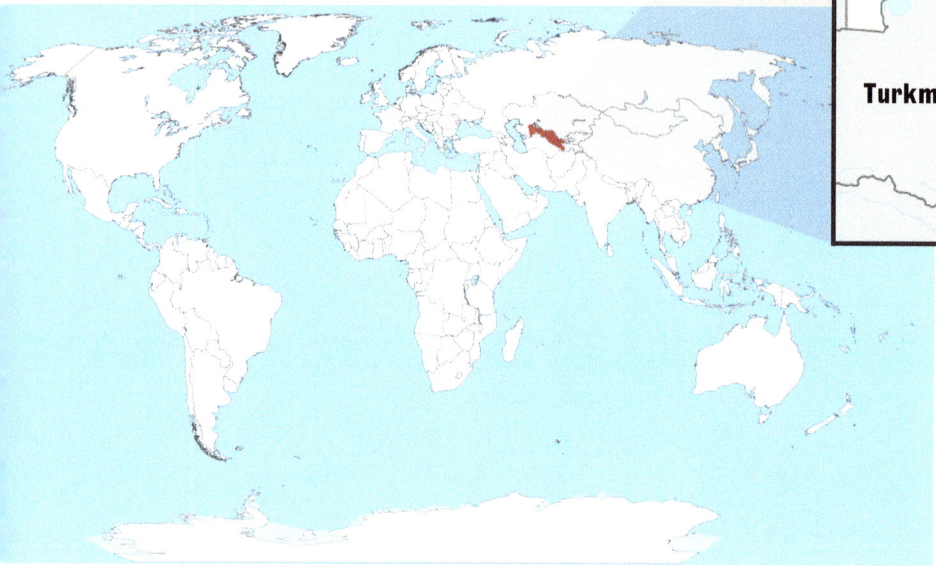

COVER BY

CHY Illustration & Design

The Proud Muslim Kids series by Green Fig is designed to engagingly teach youngsters basic concepts of Islam in a way that speaks to their hearts and minds. Each book in the series is crafted by a staff of qualified educators, writers, illustrators, parents and children. Not only is the Proud Muslim Kids series designed to supplement the early childhood and elementary Islamic curriculum, it is a great addition to any school or home library. Covering a wide variety of topics such as the Five Pillars of Islam, Islamic culture, and Islamic history, parents and children will return to these books and enjoy them together time and time again.